As I Hold You and Kiss You Goodnight

ISBN 979-8-88540-607-9 (paperback)
ISBN 979-8-88540-608-6 (digital)

Christian Faith Publishing
832 Park Avenue
Meadville, PA 16335
www.christianfaithpublishing.com

Printed in the United States of America

As I Hold You and Kiss You Goodnight

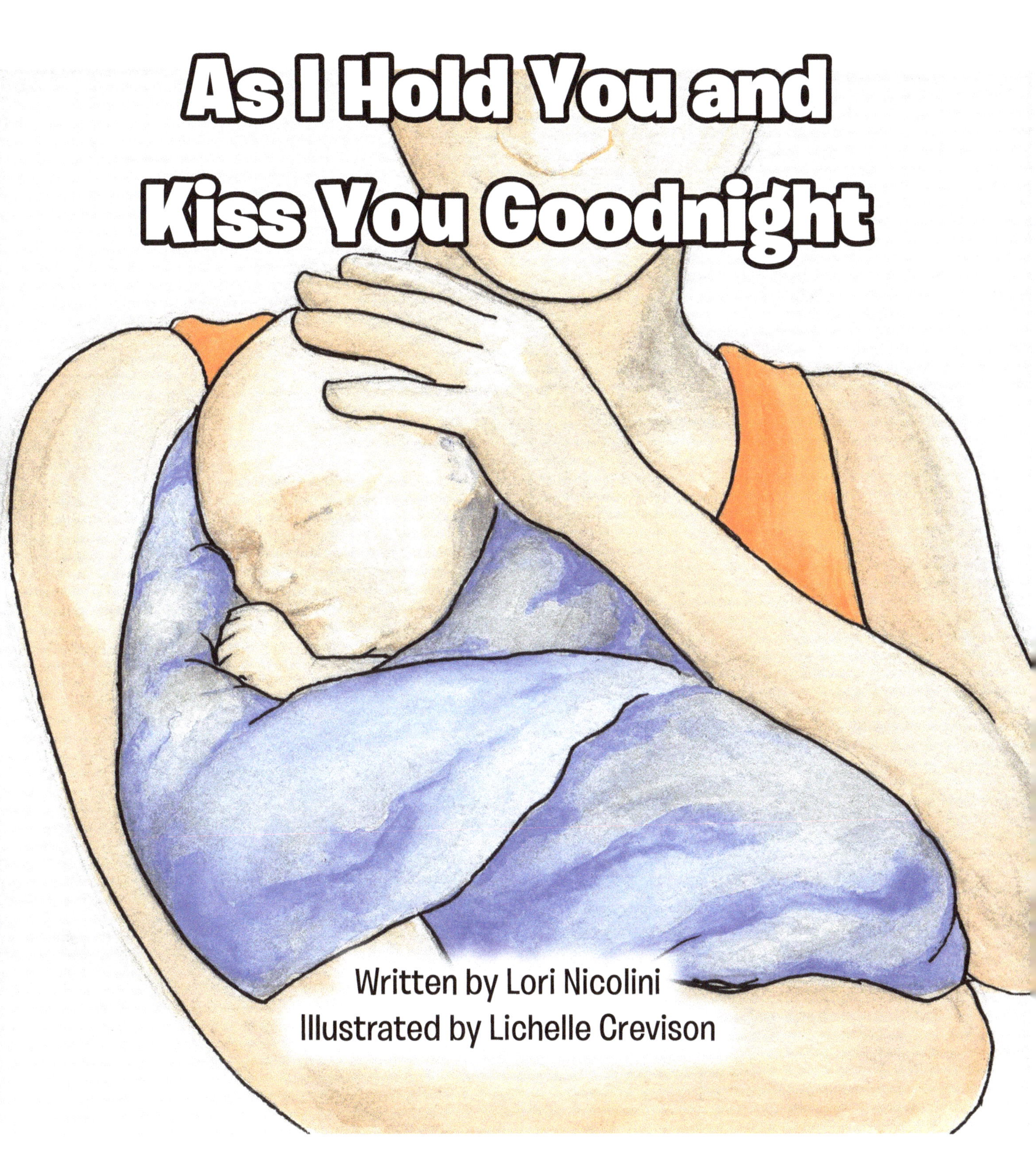

Written by Lori Nicolini

Illustrated by Lichelle Crevison

The moment that I knew you began to exist
Is when I made my decision to commit.

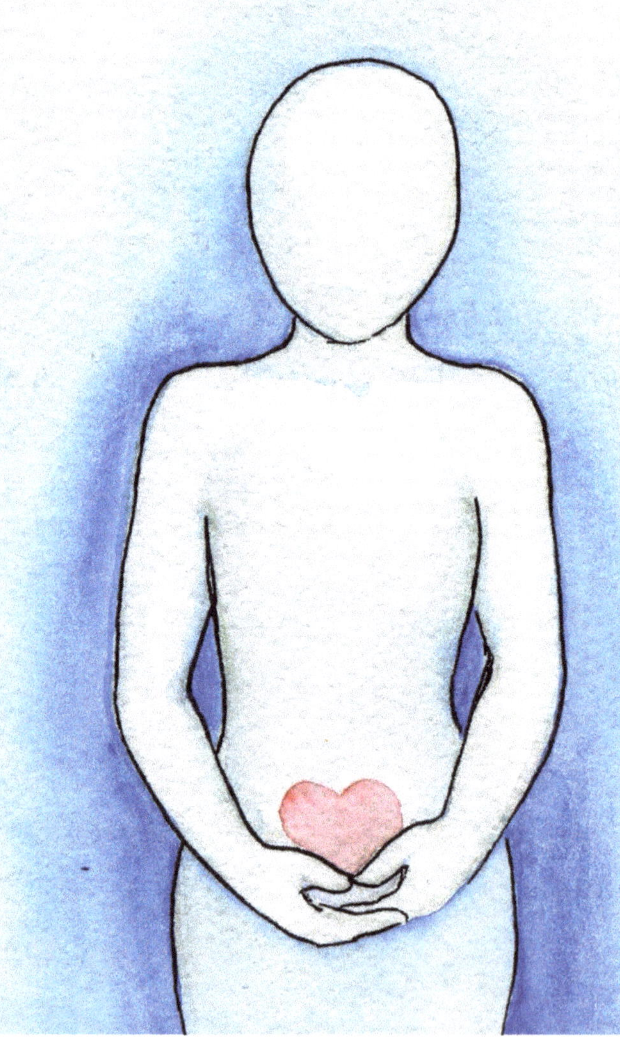

1

Such a unique moment in time
When I realized you are truly all mine.

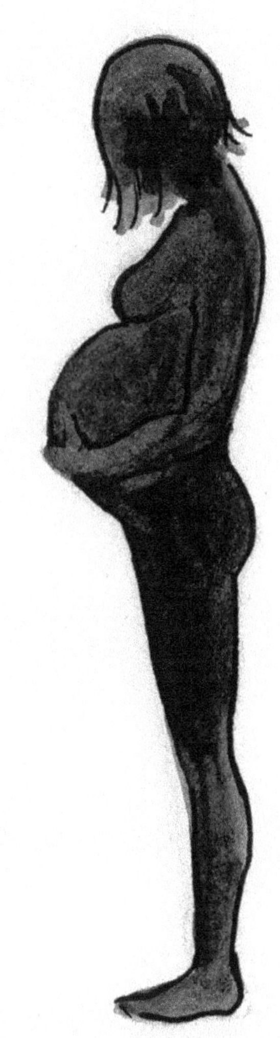

A long journey of nourishment
and transition
Has placed me in a foreign condition.

While taking your comfortable position,
My tummy grows larger as you come to fruition.

Nestled so tight in my ever-growing vessel,
Developing traits that will make you so special.

Tired and restless as I near the end of this phase
When you will be ready to reveal and amaze.

I can't even fathom the moment we meet
When we look in each other's eyes and greet.

A moment anticipated with
a touch of great fear,
"Will I be a good mother?" as you draw near.

While you poke and prod
from the internal,
I can only think of my
next hurdle.

9

Will I give exactly what you need
While I try to figure it out and proceed?

I promise to hold you and
snuggle you tight
as I wake with you
several times a night.

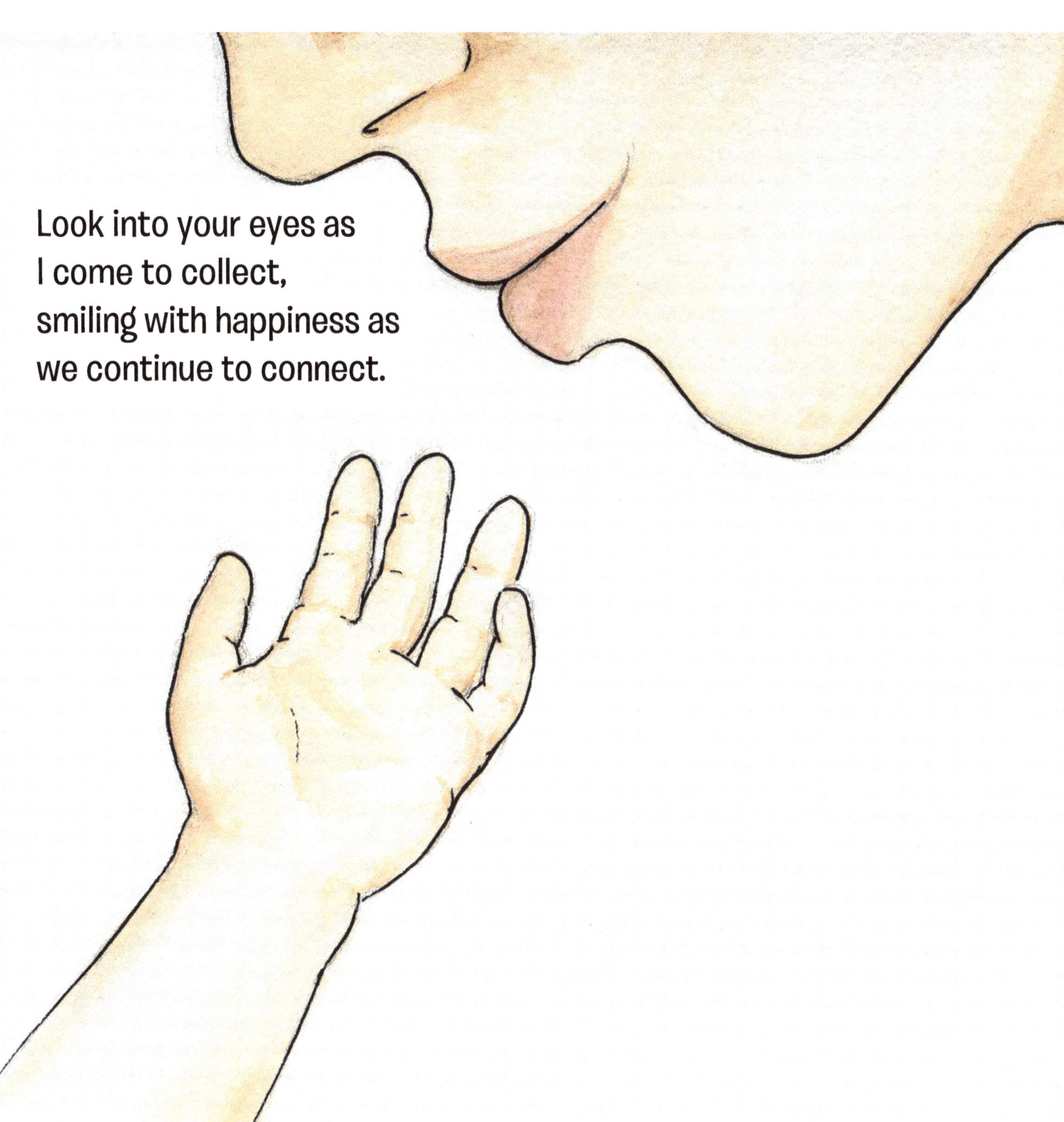

Look into your eyes as
I come to collect,
smiling with happiness as
we continue to connect.

Sing, read, laugh, and smile
as we lay swaddled together a while.

Let you rest upon my chest
as I ease you to sleep with my caress.

Watch you slowly drift off to sleep,
amazed you already have my heart to keep.

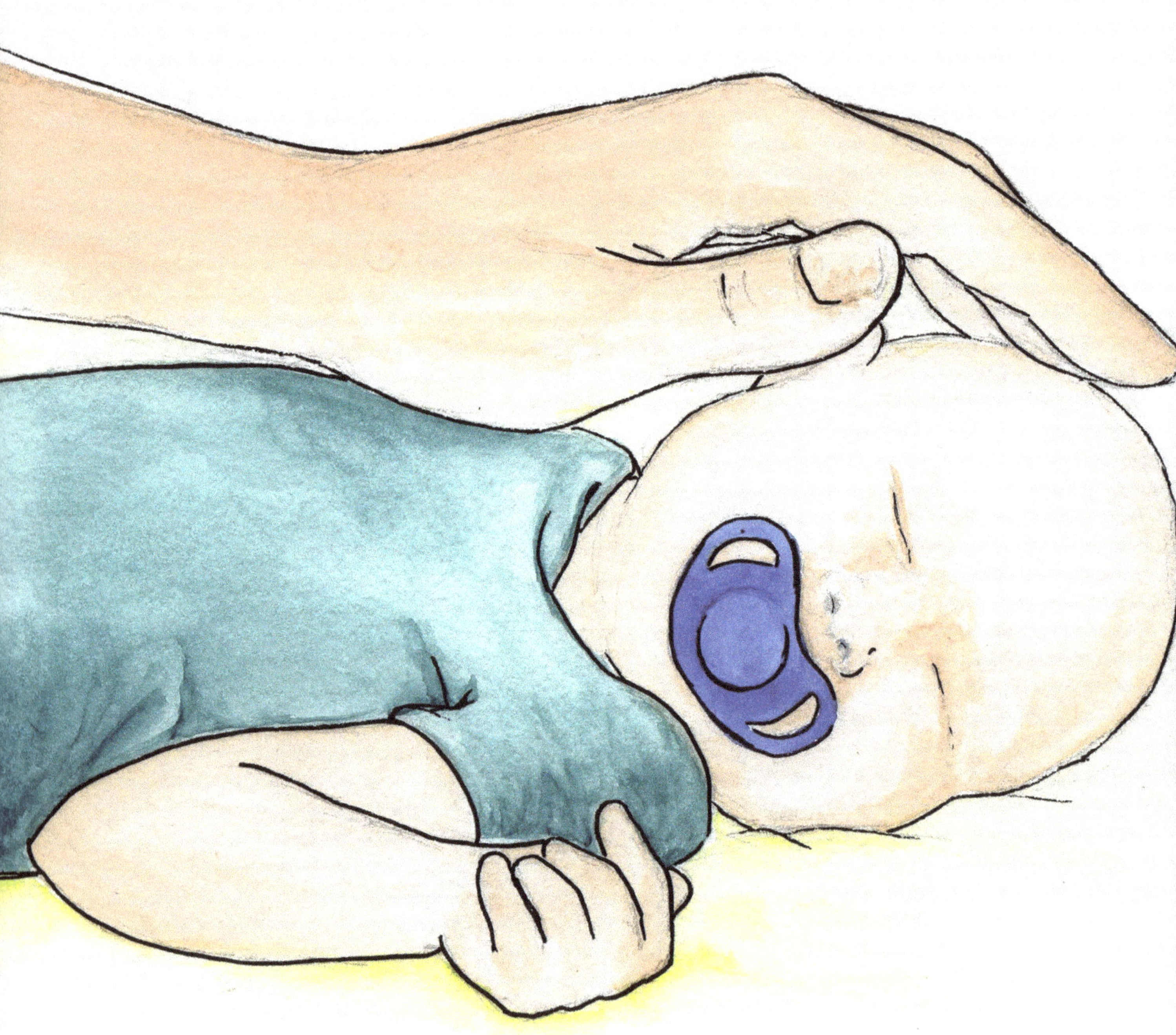

15

When you wake
and call for me,
I will be there
indefinitely.

Our bond that started inside my tummy
Grew wild with your existence bestowed upon me.

A new companion with great expectation
For me to provide with every inclination.

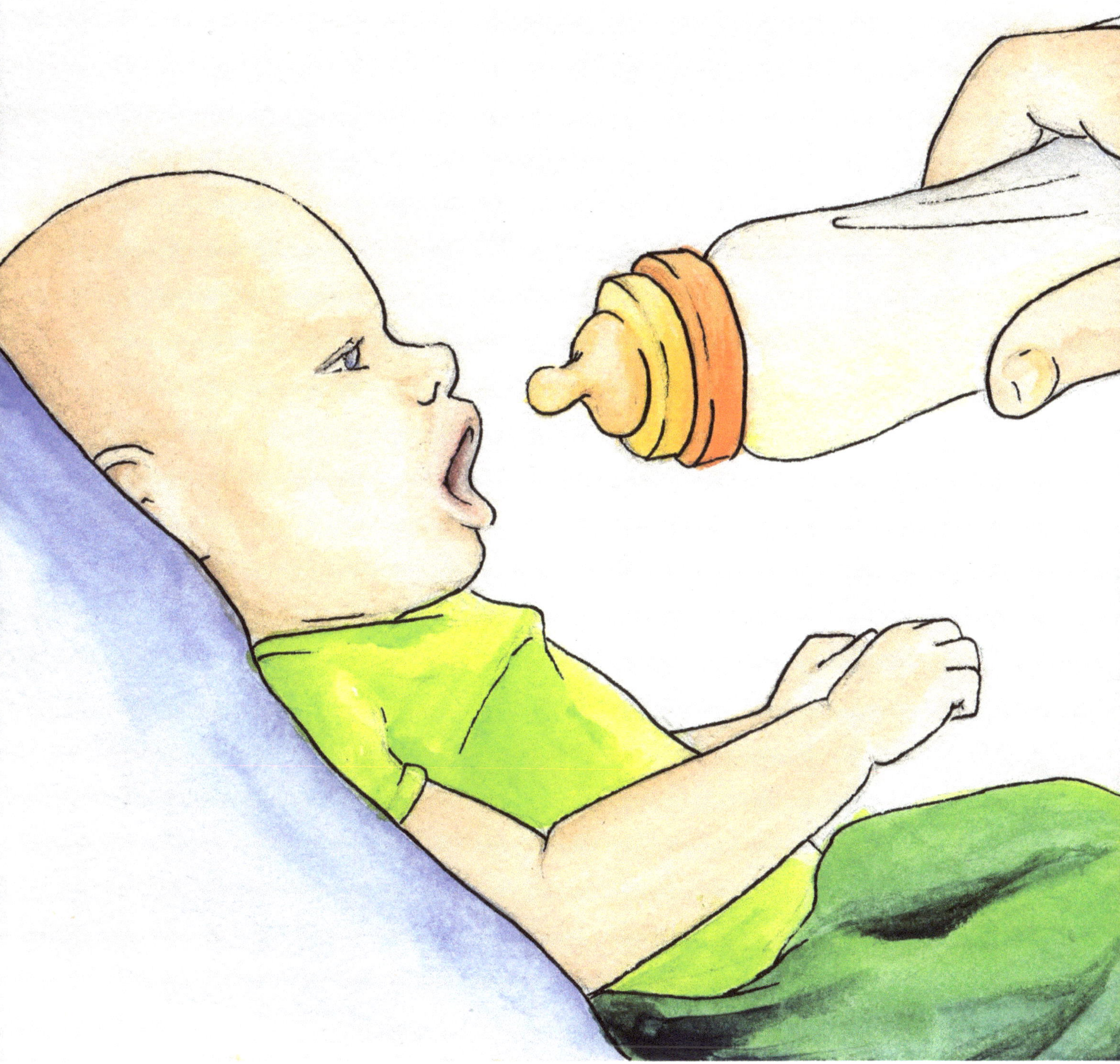

With you there is no point in negotiation.

For I will give you whatever you want with acclamation.

To provide you with comfort will become my destiny

To teach you how to love openly.

To reach beyond your means with every endeavor.

To watch as you
become more
and more clever.

To be there when you feel you're falling apart.

To tell you to always trust in your heart.

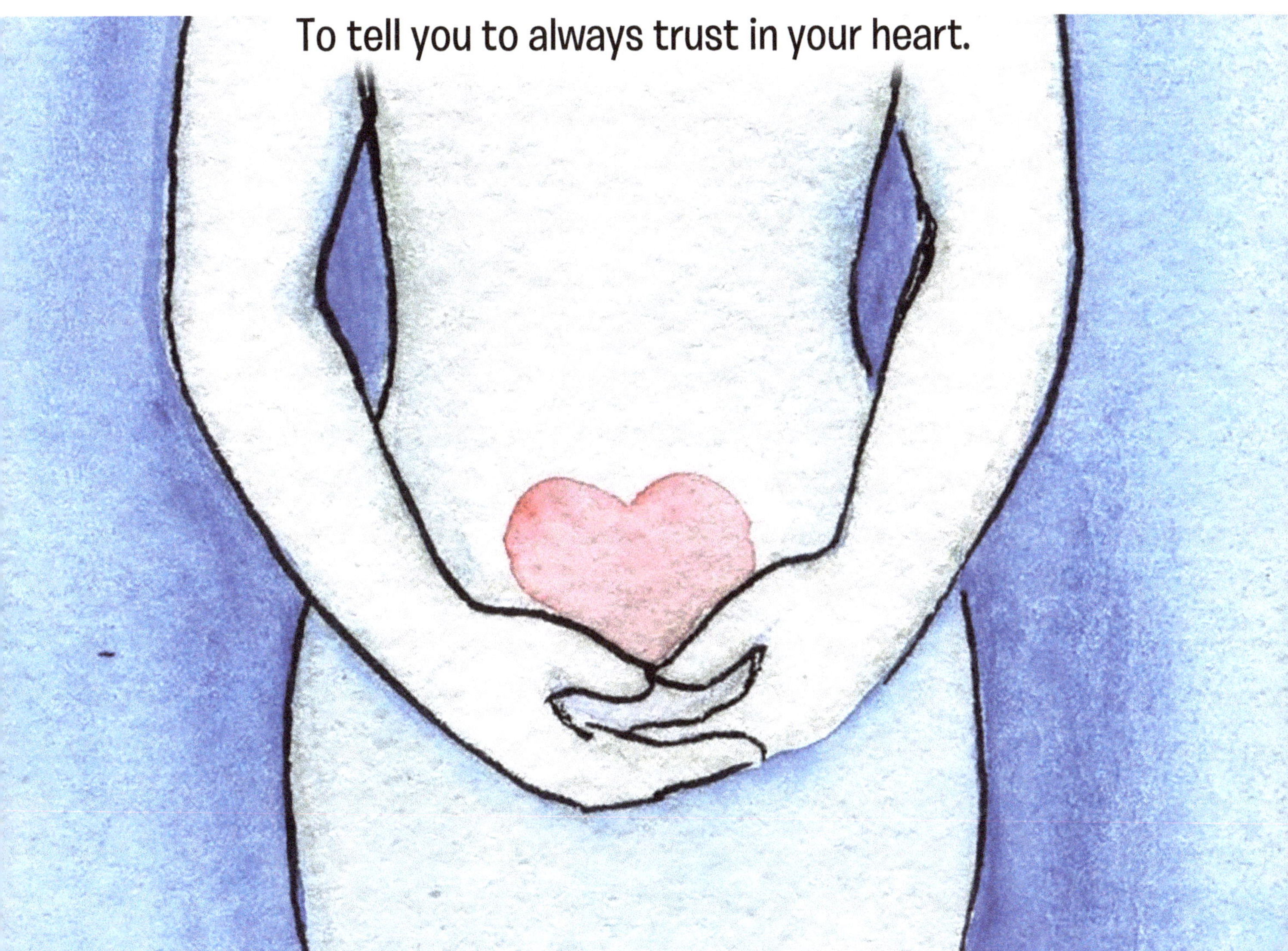

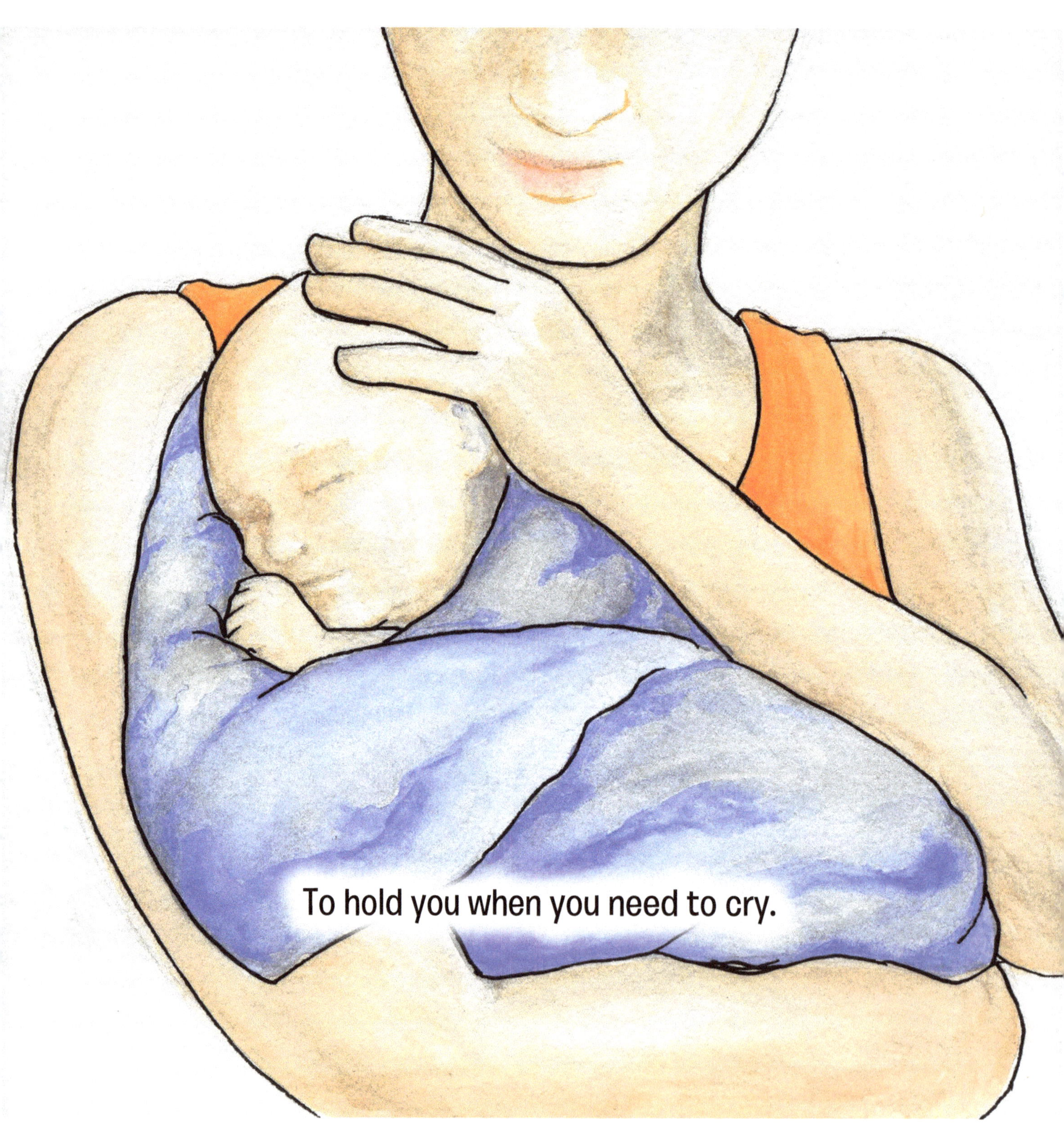

To hold you when you need to cry.

To let you go when you say goodbye.

To listen when you need an ear.

To let you know I will always be here.

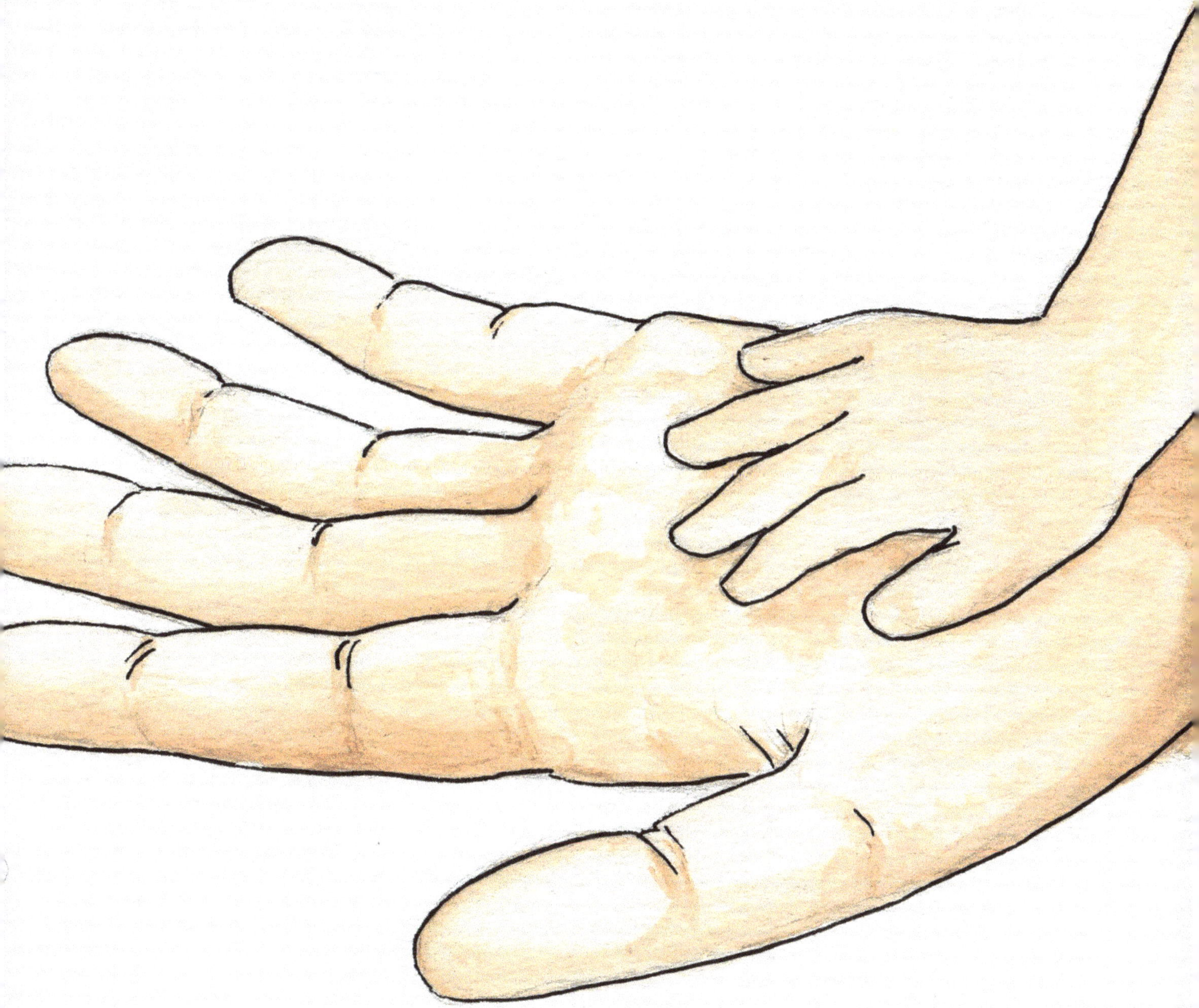

From my tummy now into my
arms has given me reason
To wake every day and
welcome each season.

Without words, you express the love we share
As your eyes emanate all the love you declare.

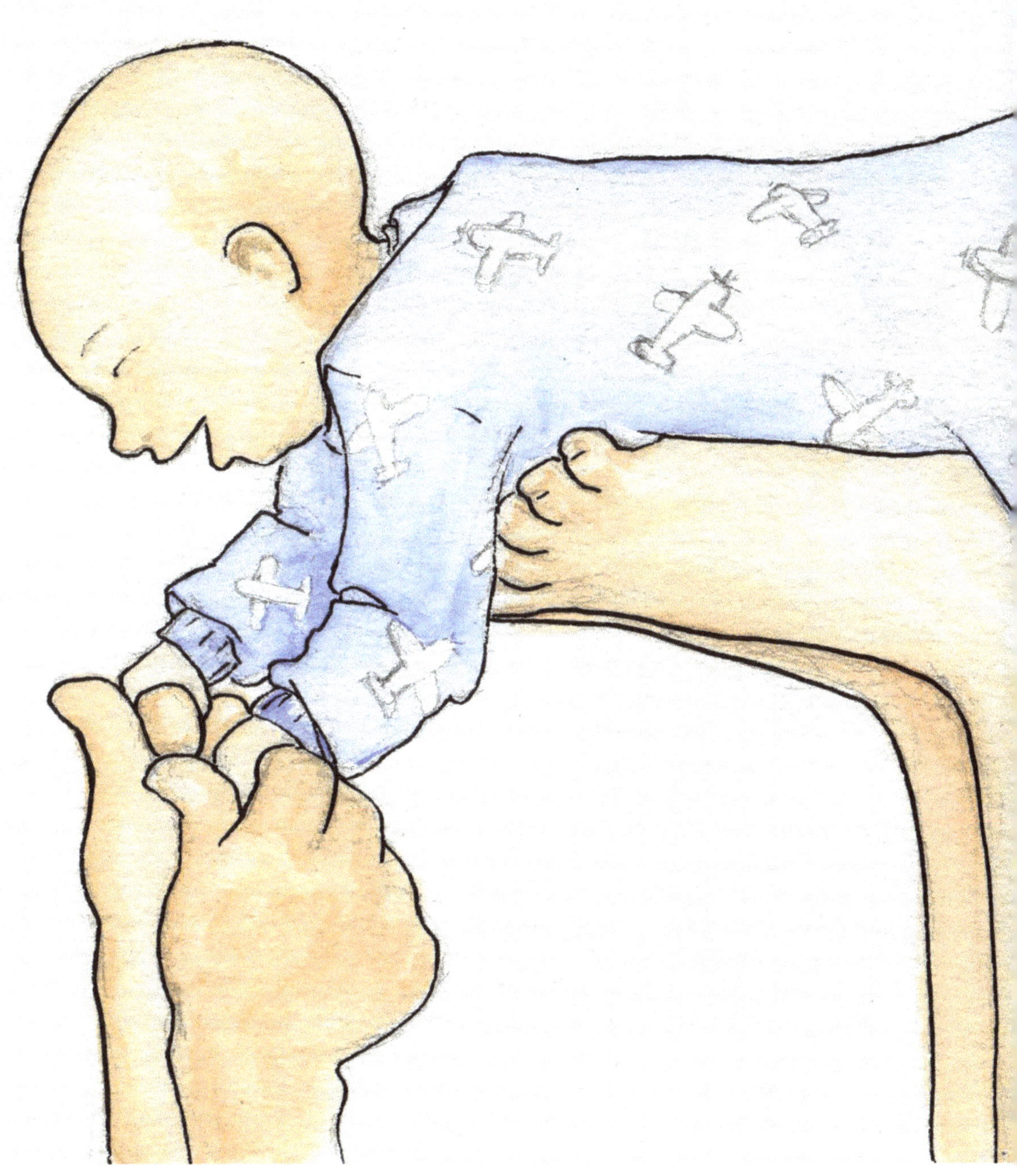

I give you my whole heart
with nothing to spare.
Together, we will take over
the world without a care.

What started as one
has now become
a pair
Connected
by love
extending
everywhere.

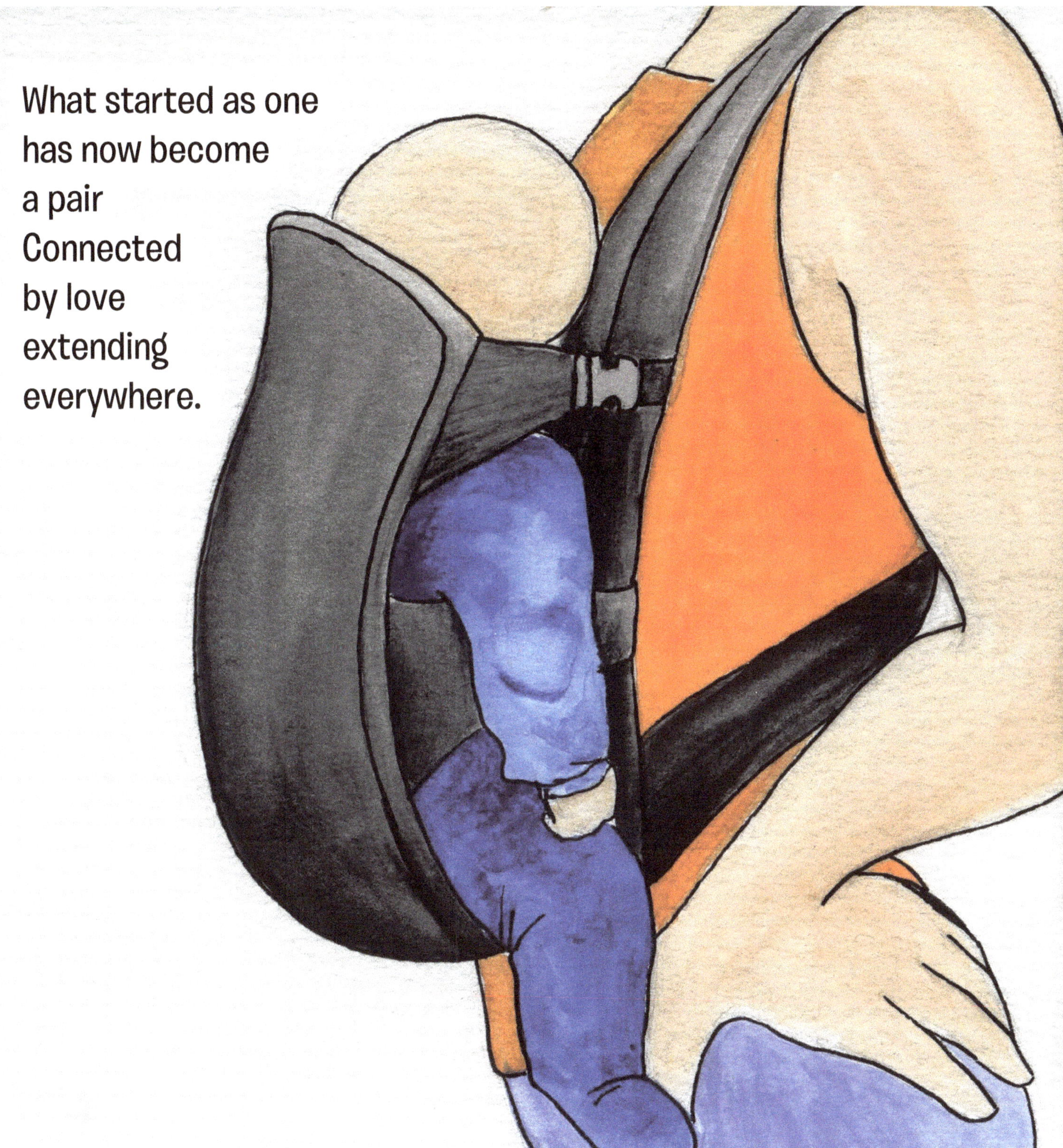

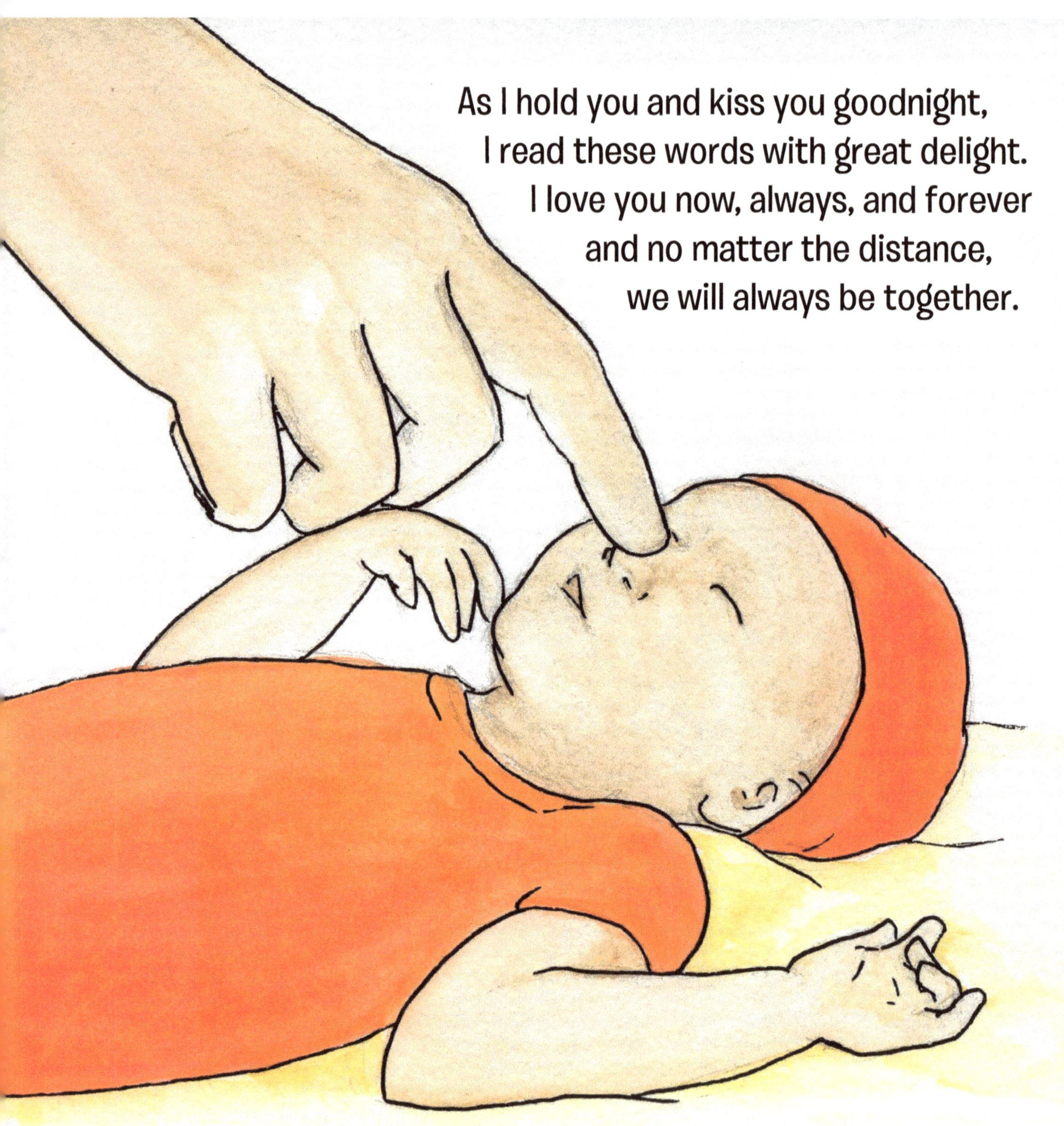

As I hold you and kiss you goodnight,
I read these words with great delight.
I love you now, always, and forever
and no matter the distance,
we will always be together.

About the Author

Lori Nicolini is a lover of all things beautiful, inspiring, and that make her laugh. She finds much inspiration through walks in nature with her very playful Irish wolfhound-Lab mix, Athena, and spending quality time with her amazing son, Aydan. Her passion lies in creating photographs of people and places while writing stories and poetry that speak from the heart and move the mind. She also enjoys rollerblading, Spartan races, yoga, meditating, and traveling. It would never be out of place to find Lori dancing at a club or festival, making a fuss over an animal, singing karaoke, or playing a competitive game like *Big Buck Hunter* into a championship competition. On a more quiet day, you may find her in a coffee shop or strolling in an art gallery.

Lori's favorite author of children's books, whom she greatly admires, is Dr. Seuss. One of her favorite quotes of the late Dr. Seuss she refers to regularly as a parent is this: "Children want the same things we want. To laugh, to be challenged, to be entertained, and delighted."

She strongly believes in feathering the lines between children and adults as much as possible for them to be present together in each moment and nurture the inner child of all souls. She is delighted to continue creating her children's series and sharing all the fun and excitement of being a parent as you join her on this journey.